INTERCOURSE WITH SUPERIOR MINDS

A Means To A Best Life Possible

---

by

ANTHONY ODERINDE

Founder of pathtorealpossibility.com

Published by

Life Advancement Incorporation
6, Larchwood Avenue
Manchester, M9 4QS, UK

ISBN -13: 978-1-9999992-0-9

Contents

Introduction

What are you really after my friend? Do you want more money, better relationship, and love? Do you want happiness, peace of mind, and accomplish much more in your career or business? Are you just starting out and you want to discover your purpose and passion in life?

Whatever it is you are after, the one action on your part that will guarantee success and produce desire results is for you to begin at once to have regular intercourse with superior minds.

There are millions of outstanding and brilliant minds who have walked this path before us who have achieved profound success in every walks of life. They have done what you are trying to do and have made success of it and you can just follow in their footstep.

Even in those things we call new invention, they have in the least set the ball rolling somehow and all you need to do is build on what they have started. The truth according to the bible is:

"The thing which hath been, is that which shall be; and that which has been done is that which shall be done: and there is no new thing under the sun."

The wise men of the past and present have always admonished us whatever our area of calling, to take to books, for they are the windows through which the soul looks out. Books are the bridges between the past and the present. They have literally raised the poor out of the dust, and lifted the beggar from the dunghill, to set them among princes.

Do you ever think there is any power on earth who would have opened the door to the White House to the poor, awkward backwoods boy called Lincoln, if he had not immersed himself in books, prepared and developed himself to the utmost those qualities which make men leaders?

You cannot keep a determined, ambitious youth who have taken solace in books from success. Put stumbling blocks in his way and he takes them as stepping stones. Take away his money but give him his books, and he will turn the situation around. Put him in a log cabin in the wilderness, and one day, you will find him in the White House.

No wonder Cicero said that he would part with all he was worth so he might live and die among his books," says Geikie. FENELON obviously understood the divine power of books when he said "If the crowns of all the kingdoms of the empire were laid down at my feet in exchange for my books and my love of reading, I would spurn them all"

As I study my books says Sir William Waller, I can call up the ablest spirits, the most learned philosophers, the wisest counsellors, the greatest generals, and make them serviceable to me.

One by one, men of achievement have gathered from all departments of human learning multitude of books. They understand books are not alabaster vases filled with the sweetest perfume of the human soul, but are living creatures, they are companions; they have received the homage of our best hours.

No other thing has such power as that possessed by books to lift the poor out of his poverty, the wretched out of his misery, to make the burden-bearer forget his burden, the sick his suffering, the sorrowful his grief, the downtrodden his degradation.

Books are friends to the lonely, companions to the deserted, joy to the joyless, hope to the hopeless, good cheer to the disheartened, a helper to the helpless. They bring light into darkness, and sunshine into shadow.

We may temporarily be poor, socially ostracized and shut out from all personal association with the great and the good, and yet be in the best society in the world, in books. Possessing them, we may live in palaces, converse with princes, be familiar with royalty, and associate with the greatest and noblest of all time.

Happy is the man" says Alexander Cockburn, "who, when the day's work is done, finds his rest and solace and recreation in communion with the master minds of the present and of the past, —in study, and in literature

All that man has ever thought, felt, experienced, or done, lives in books for there is no past so long as books shall live. Nations rise and fall, great cities are buried in ruins, vast empires obliterated, but the whole past lives in books.

Make good use of them and thou shall be wise

PART ONE

Books And Superior Minds

Chapter 1

Spare Moment with Einstein

The great sage "Amos Bronson Alcott" said: "*That is a good book which is opened with expectation, and closed with delight and profit.*" Another wise man "Carlyle" said: "*The true university of these days is a collection of books.*"

God be thanked for books. They are the voices of the distant and the dead, and make us heirs of the spiritual life of past ages. Books are true levelers. They give, to all who will faithfully use them, the society, the spiritual presence, of the best and greatest of our race.

It does not matter how poor I am, it does not even matter if the prosperous and noble of my own time will refuse to enter my obscure dwelling, if the sacred writers will enter and take up their abode under my roof.

If Milton will cross my threshold to sing to me of Paradise, and Shakespeare will open to me the worlds of imagination and the workings of the human mind. If Franklin will enrich me with his practical wisdom and I can spend my spare moments with Einstein, I shall not mourn or grieve for want of intellectual companionship, and I may become a cultivated man, though excluded from what is called the best society in the place where I live.

(WILLIAM ELLERY CHANNING)

When I consider what some books have done for the world, and what they are doing, how they keep up our hope, awaken new courage and faith, soothe pain, give an ideal life to those whose homes are hard and cold, bind together distant ages and foreign lands, create new worlds of beauty, bring down truths from heaven, I give eternal blessings for this gift.

(JAMES FREEMAN CLARKE)

The account of Lincoln

There are no better gifts as books. They have time and time again lifted up the poor out of their poverty and slaves out of their slavery and placed them among the noble to the amazement of people around. It was this power that lifted Lincoln from his common old log cabin and placed him on the highest throne.

On the old floorless and windowless log cabin, we see young Lincoln lie on the ground, devouring by the light of the fire, as if he might never see it again, the *"Life of Washington,"* and other precious volumes, which he has walked many miles to borrow, for he cannot afford to own even one.

There were no libraries in that wilderness, and very few cabins contain any book, except the Bible. See this boy, thirsting for knowledge, his soul fired by the few books he has walked to Springfield and back to borrow and return, sitting up till long after midnight, and rising before daylight, to dip into the precious volumes whose scenes have haunted his dreams.

With the *"Life of Washington"* in it, his humble cabin seems a paradise. With brain-expanded, mind cultured, and character improved as a results of the volumes of books he had consumed, no power on earth could stand between him and the white house.

The Account of Booker T. Washington

The unseen power on the pages of books lifted a slave boy to the table of presidents Theodore Roosevelt and William Howard Taft.

Booker T Washington in his own words:

I was born a slave on a plantation in Franklin County, Virginia. My life had its beginning in the midst of the most miserable, desolate, and discouraging surroundings.

One day, while at work in the coal-mine, I happened to overhear two miners talking about a great school for colored people somewhere in Virginia.

As they went on describing the school, it seemed to me that it must be the greatest place on earth, and not even Heaven presented more attractions for me at that time than did the Hampton Normal and Agricultural Institute in Virginia, about which these men were talking.

I resolved at once to go to that school, although I had no idea where it was, or how many miles away, or how I was going to reach it; I remembered only that I was on fire constantly with one ambition, and that was to go to Hampton. This thought was with me day and night.

Before I went to Hampton, I took up an employment with Mrs. Ruffner. During the one or two winters that I was with her she gave me an opportunity to go to school for an hour in the day during a portion of the winter months, but most of my studying was done at night, sometimes alone, sometimes under someone whom I could hire to teach me.

It was while living with Mrs. Ruffner that I began to get together my first library. I secured a dry-goods box, knocked out one side of it, put some shelves in it, and began putting into it every kind of book that I could get my hands upon, and called it my "library."

With brain-expanded, mind cultured, and character improved as a result of books, Booker T Washington went on to become a notable figure and eventually became political adviser to president Theodore Roosevelt and president William Howard Taft.

The unseen power on the pages of books

Desirable books produce a doubly good result; they inspire noble thoughts and build high ideals, while leaving no room, for pernicious literature. A thing to be remembered is that young people are bound to read something. It usually remains with their parents or guardians whether this something shall be helpful or harmful.

If the books chosen are good and noble, the unseen power between the pages will lift the reader up beyond his or her wildest dream to the paradise of greatness and achievement. If the books on the other hand are of low quality and immoral, this same power will pull down the reader to hell, the land of failure and despondency.

The man who spends all he earns for rich food, costly raiment, and unnecessary decoration, and provides no mental and moral stimulant in the way of reading, purchases almost inevitable disaster, and fails to acquire a mighty force for good.

"No entertainment is so cheap as reading," says Mary Wortley Montagu; "nor any other pleasure so lasting." Good books elevate the character, purify the taste, and lift us to a higher plane of thinking and living. It is not easy to be mean directly after reading a noble and inspiring book.

Inestimable compensation for a well-read mind

Educating one's mind through the treasures on the pages of books will pay in morals, manners, and good, hard cash, for the rightly educated person is the person who is everywhere wanted in positions that pay well.

But, someone may say, like thousands of others, I cannot afford a bookcase, to say nothing of books to fill one. I seriously doubt this, but assuming this is indeed true, be sure you secure at least one good book once every three months, for there is hardly a person who cannot, in these days of inexpensive publications, do this, and that one good book is your own food and subject of conversation for the three months' period.

Do you think one book can do little good? If you can read the stories of the great minds who shake the world, you will find that it was not the reading of many books, but reading over and over and absorbing and digesting the matter of a few books, or in more than one instance of only one, that started these giants on their upward way.

You will also find, that the seeing or reading of one bad book in youth has caused many souls to take the downward path. A book that starts a young person on a life career is a great power. The inspiration of a single book has made teachers, preachers, philosophers, authors and statesmen. On the other hand, the demoralizing effect of one book has made infidels, profligates, and criminals.

The account of Napoleon

Ossian's poems had a marked impression on Napoleon's life, and he was never weary of singing the praises of Homer. "He always, even in his most hurried campaigns, took a compact library with him," says John S. C. Abbott. When driving in his carriage from post to post of the army, he improved the moments in garnering up that knowledge for the accumulation of which he ever manifested such an insatiable desire.

He devoured biography, history, philosophy, treatises upon political economy and upon all the sciences. His contempt for works of fiction, the whole class of novels and romances, amounted almost to indignation. He could never endure to see one reading such a book, or to have such a volume in his presence.

Once, in passing through the salons of his palace, he found one of the maids of honor with a novel in her hands. He took it from her, gave her a severe lecture for wasting her time in such frivolous reading, and cast the volume into the flames. When he had a few moments for diversion, he employed them in looking over a book of logarithms, in which he always found recreation."

Great Minds whose lives were influenced by books

Cotton Mather's "Essay to Do Good" helped to shape Franklin's whole career. Tyndall was greatly influenced by

Emerson's book on "Nature." Beecher declares that Ruskin's books taught him the secret of seeing, and that no man could ever again be quite the same man or look at the world in the same way after reading them.

Madame Roland would take a copy of Plutarch's "Lives" to church, and read a sentence at every pause in the devotional exercises. The book was also a favorite with Napoleon. Shakespeare copied many things from Plutarch, sometimes repeating his language word for word.

Curran used to read Homer through once a year. The sight of an engraving representing Troy in flames, its battlements clearly defined, stimulated Dr. Schliemann to attempt those explorations and excavations which have resulted in such wonderful discoveries. Luther was encouraged by the life and writings of John Huss.

Thinking of what books have done and how many great men and women they have produced, I believe parents do not need to wait for prophets or seers to tell them the importance of equipping their children with good books.

But some will probably complain that their trouble is to make their children read at all. They seem utterly indifferent to everything in printed form. An excellent article on this subject appeared from the pen of Marguerite Brooks, who said:

Much well-meant advice has been given on the subject of reading; innumerable pages have been printed telling how, and how not, what, and what not, to read; and endless lists of the best hundred books.

But, for the boy or girl who has not inherited, or been born with, a love for reading, there is little advice or suggestion. The happiness and success of boys and girls of this class lie to a great extent in the hands of the teachers; for, if their parents have themselves a love for reading, they will try to create a taste for it in their children.

The easy way to introduce children into the world of reading

One can hardly estimate what an all-important influence early reading has on the present development and future life of a child. The dull boy or the one who has no taste for reading, must be introduced to books gently, and skillfully, must be beguiled into reading, as it were, unconsciously, of his own choice.

To recommend books, to put one into his hand, or to tell him he should or must read this or that, would be about as effectual as leading an unwilling horse to drink, or trying to whip a lazy boy into a recognition of the beauty and utility of work. Endeavor, rather, to excite his curiosity or interest by relating incidents from the works of the best writers of prose and poetry, beginning with those suited to his understanding.

Make him acquainted with the famous Queen Scheherazade, who saved her life and won the heart of the tyrannical sultan of the Indies, by the wonderful series of stories that she wove for his entertainment, from night to night.

Then awaken his imagination by a brief sketch of 'Hiawatha,' the story of 'Evangeline,' or 'The Pilgrim's Progress.' The choice of mental food is almost unlimited. But be sure that whatever you choose is entertaining, as well as instructive and uplifting. "Do not give to the dull boy, or, indeed to any boy, goody-goody stories, or books that round every paragraph with a moral.

Children, whether bright or dull, do not enjoy being preached at any more than do their elders. Neither should their intellectual diet be of the mushy order, too babyish to stimulate thought or quicken attention.

Catch them young

It is too little understood by parents and teachers, that even children not yet in their teens have an appreciation of noble sentiment and heroic action, and that an acquaintance with the masterpieces of literature should not be deferred until they go to high school or college.

An excellent way to arouse the interest of a dull boy is to read aloud thrilling selections, both in prose and poetry, passages that stir the blood and appeal even to the most sluggish intellect by their tenderness or daring.

The Bible, Shakespeare, Milton's 'Paradise Lost, Tennyson's 'Idylls of the King,' or 'In Memoriam'; 'David Copperfield' and a host of other good books which can be find in the kid's section of any book's store, will furnish admirable matter for this purpose.

But the stimulating process must not be confined to fairy-tales, poetry, and fiction. In the same way the child may be led, stage by stage, to enjoy history, books of travel, stories of invention and discovery, science, biography, even metaphysics, until he becomes a joint inheritor with all who can read of that glorious bequest of which none can rob him the treasures of the master minds of the ages.

The type of reading to guard against

There is one kind of reading that should be steadily guarded against, —the hop-skip-and-jump style, that one may get through a great many books merely for the sake of saying he has read them. I once heard of a young woman, who, in confidence, told a friend that she read reviews of all the new books, so that in company she could appear to have read the books themselves.

You make a great mistake, replied the candid friend. First you sow a habit of deceit, which is bad and disintegrating for any character. Secondly, you acquire a habit of skimming, which is disastrous to helpful or the most enjoyable reading.

Thirdly, you plant in your mind the idea that you are under some sort of obligation to read all the new books. Why, you might as well and as healthily try to taste all the foods in a restaurant as even to dip into all the new books.

One would ruin your physical, the other your literary, if not your moral, digestion, and leave you unable to digest and assimilate wholesome food for body or mind."

Hasty reading, superficial reading, overtaxes the memory until it loses its power to grasp and hold. The mind loses its focusing power, the power to bring together and to compare, its power of close attention and continuity of thought, without which no great intellectual work can ever be accomplished.

Elizabeth Barrett Browning said, "We go wrong by reading too much, and out of proportion to what we think. It is said that Harriet Martineau read only a page in an hour. Edmund

Burke always so read a book as to make it his own, a possession for life.

The mere acquisition of unrelated facts contributes very little to a real education. One may have a limitless command of dates and figures and statistics, and still have a mind unformed and incapable of reasoning.

Read less of newspapers and more of good books

I do not have any grudge against the editors of newspapers, but there is no doubt at all that the tendency of the mass of readers nowadays is to waste time in reading disconnected paragraphs, news, or statements of fact, or bits of description, and this tendency is stimulated by the make-up of newspapers.

It is true that many items of news must of necessity be brief, a mere mention of incidents more or less important and interesting. But the papers do not stop with this, but print whole columns of little paragraphs, which may or may not contain 'useful information,' but, being wholly unrelated, add nothing to the general education.

As the mental, like the physical, appetite grows by what it feeds on, the tendency of this kind of reading is to destroy one's interest in anything but scraps. The intellectual powers are dissipated, and the taste for that severe and consecutive study which alone trains and develops the mind, is diminished by daily devotion to trifles.

This is not the only evil, it happens that a very considerable proportion of the news of the day is made up of crimes and disasters. It is perhaps inevitable that it should be so. It is the duty of the news correspondents to report incidents, and, as they must report briefly, crimes and accidents constitute the mass of incidents, and, taking the world over a very large mass, they make up a great part of the daily history.

What the average purchaser of a newspaper wants is the unusual and the exciting story that gratify the emotion, not how his bad eating habit is likely to affect his general health condition or how he or she is to get more done through a discipline lifestyle. He seeks a few minutes of distraction from the rather benumbing influence of his daily toil.

The editors of course understand this unquenchable appetite of many, so he prints the crimes and disasters, and, of course, as compilers of current history, to a certain extent justified in doing so; for, as there is a good deal in our civilization that is bad and distressing, it should, within bounds, be made public.

Now, suppose our race to have passed away leaving nothing behind but its newspapers, what would be the impression they would make upon the future of the coming generation, as to the character of our civilization? Yet it would be much the same impression that a long course of newspaper paragraphs leaves upon the reader, a feeling that bloodthirst and disaster and misfortune fill all human life.

As reading the same thing day after day does in the end influence mind and character, the effect of a long course of these 'incidents' can be very disastrous. True, the reader in a measure may be able to protect himself by consciously shutting out the feelings but in the long run they do deflect his mind from its right course, and lower his conception of the world's progress.

As energy depends a good deal upon cheerfulness, such a result cannot be good. It is not well to look constantly on the dark side of life, to realize how prone human nature is to evil, and how little safe guard there is against misfortune.

Personal Library – a necessity

There is something in the very atmosphere of books which is helpful and inspiring to everyone. The mind changes; our ideals enlarge, when we are surrounded by good books. One can learn to love books, too, by constantly being in the presence of them, and by getting acquainted with them. There is a very satisfactory feeling about the books one owns; he may linger over them, lend them, or do with them as he pleases.

Probably much of the wisdom which most people possess came from things which they read and re-read many times in their schoolbooks. The sense of hurry engendered by the knowledge that a book must be returned to the public library at a certain time is extremely detrimental, if not fatal, to that absorption of its meaning from which alone can come power or restful pleasure.

Therefore, have a library of your own. It needs not be a large library. Nearly all the greatest men and women in the world history read but few books when young, but these few they read so exhaustively, and digested so thoroughly, that their spirit, purpose, and principles became a part of the readers' very souls, the dynamos which moved their lives to great ends.

Start a library, no matter how small it may be at first. Make a start. Cover each volume; get a small bookcase, if possible, and add to your books as rapidly as possible. They will promote your mental health.

To rummage around among books, reading a few pages here and a few pages there, without thought or aim, is worse than wasting time, worse than ignorance which comes from reading nothing, for we are forming desultory habits, which are fatal to continuity of thought.

PART TWO

Books And Life Purpose

Chapter 2

Discover your purpose through Reading

I know of nothing else which will enlarge one's ideals and lift one's life standards more than the study of the lives of great and noble characters; the reading of biographies of great men and women.

Abroad, it is impossible for me to avoid the society of fools. In my study, I can call up the ablest spirits, the most learned philosophers, the wisest counsellors, the greatest generals, and make them serviceable to me.

(Sir William Waller)

The real purpose of reading is for self-discovery. Inspirational, character-making, life-shaping books are helpful for discovering one's life purpose. There are books that have raised the ideals and materially influenced entire nations. Who can estimate the value of books that give rise to ambition, that awaken slumbering possibilities?

Cotton Mather's " Essay to Do Good " influenced the whole career of Benjamin Franklin, we are told. Will you like to associate with people who will inspire you to nobler deeds? then begin to read uplifting books, which will stir you to make the most of yourself.

We all know how completely changed we sometimes are after reading a book which has taken a strong, vigorous hold upon us. Thousands of people have found themselves through the reading of some book which has opened the door within them and given them the first glimpse of their possibilities.

There are men and women in our society whose whole lives have been shaped, the entire trend of their careers completely changed, uplifted beyond their fondest dreams, by the good books they have taken time to read.

It was rightly said by President White of Cornell that, " The great thing that needed to be taught to everyone is truth, simple ethics, the distinction between right and wrong. Stress should be laid upon what is best in biography, upon noble deeds and sacrifices, especially those which show that the greatest man is not the greatest orator, or the tricky politician.

What we need are noble men. National loss comes as the penalty for frivolous boyhood and girlhood, that gains no moral stamina from wholesome books.

If youths learn to feed on the thoughts of the great men and women of all times, they will never again be satisfied with the common or low; they will never again be contented with mediocrity; they will aspire to something higher and nobler.

A day which is passed without treasuring up some good thought is not well spent. Every day is a page in the book of life. The readers who do not know the Concord philosopher Emerson, and the great writers of antiquity, Marcus Aurelius, Epictetus, and Plato, have pleasures to come.

Knowledge in different subjects produces a well-rounded mind

Aside from reading non - fiction, self-help books which are great source of inspiration and motivation for greatest achievement, biographies and books of travel are very good for mental diversion.

Then there are nature studies, and science and poetry, all affording wholesome recreation, all of an uplifting character, and some of them opening up study specialties of the highest order, as in the great range of books classified as Natural Science.

The reading and study of poetry is much like the interest one takes in the beauties of natural scenery. Much of the best poetry is indeed a poetic interpretation of nature. Whittier, Longfellow and Bryant lead their readers to look on nature with new eyes, as Ruskin opened the eyes of Henry Ward Beecher.

A great deal of the best prose is in style and sentiment of a true poetic character, lacking only the metrical form. To become familiar with Tennyson and Shakespeare and the brilliant catalogue of British poets is in itself a liberal education.

Knowledge of all kinds is placed before us in a most attractive and interesting manner. The best of the literatures of the world are found today in thousands of homes and public libraries where years ago they could only have been obtained by the rich.

What a shame it is that under such conditions as there are in the 21st century, a child should grow up ignorant, should be uneducated in the midst of such marvelous opportunities for self-improvement. Many of our greatest writers spend a vast amount of time in the drudgery of travel and investigation, in gathering material for books, articles, and magazines.

Publishers pay thousands of dollars for what a reader can get for a dollar or less. Thus the reader secures for a little, periodicals or books, the results of months and often years of hard work and investigation of our greatest writers.

There is no excuse for mediocrity in the 21st century

There is a great wealth within the reach of the poorest mechanic and day laborer in this age that kings in olden times could not possess, and that is the wealth of a well-read, well cultured mind. In this internet age, this age of cheap books and periodicals, there is no excuse for ignorance, for a coarse, untrained mind.

Today no one is so handicapped, if he has health and the use of his faculties, that he cannot possess himself of wealth that will enrich his whole life, and enable him to converse and mingle with the most cultured people. No one is so poor that it is impossible for him to lay hold of that which will broaden his mind, which will inform and improve him, and lift him out of the brute stage of existence into the godlike realm of knowledge.

A wise nation invests heavily in books and education of its citizens because it understands the money it spends on books and education, it saves in prisons and policing.

It seems like a miracle that the poorest boy can converse freely with the greatest philosophers and scientists, statesmen, warriors, authors of all time, with little expense, that the inmates of the humblest cabin may follow the stories of the nations, the epochs of history, the story of liberty, the romance of the world, and the course of human progress.

University in every home

Were you denied the privilege of a university education? well that is not a problem. Equip your home with collections of good books in the areas of your interest. Carlyle said that a collection of books is a university.

What a pity that the thousands of ambitious, energetic men and women who missed their opportunities for an education at the school age, and feel crippled by their loss, fail to catch the significance of this.

They fail to realize the tremendous cumulative possibilities of that great life-improver, that admirable substitute for a college or university education — reading. Have you just been to a well-educated, sharp-sighted employer to find work? You did not need to be at any trouble to tell him the names of the books you have read, because they have left their indelible mark upon your face and your speech.

Your pinched, starved vocabulary, your lack of polish, your slang expressions, tell him of the trash to which you have given your precious time. He knows that you have not rightly organized your hours or rub your mind with the minds of the greatest and most gifted of all time.

Truly, books are ladders through which beggars can climb up from their dunghills and the poor from their poverty to dine with princes and noble men and women.

Books are of such great importance that President Schumann of Cornell points with pride to a few books in his library which he says he bought when he was but a poor boy by going many a day without his dinner. The great German Professor Oken was not ashamed to ask Professor Agassiz to dine with him on potatoes and salt, that he might save some money for books.

King George III used to say that lawyers do not know so much more law than people of other callings, but that they know better where to find it. A practical working knowledge of how to find what is in the book world, relating to any given point, is worth a vast deal from a financial point of view.

James Freeman Clarke said "When I consider, what some books have done for the world, and what they are doing, how they keep up our hope, awaken new courage and faith, soothe pain, give an ideal of life to those whose homes are hard and cold, bind together distant ages and foreign lands, create new worlds of beauty, bring down truths from heaven, — I give eternal blessings for this gift.

PART THREE

In Books Lie The Solutions
To Human Problems

Chapter 3

Solutions to Man's Major Problems

Jim Rohn was very accurate when he said:

"All the books that we will ever need to make us as rich, as healthy, as happy, as Powerful, as sophisticated and as successful as we want to be have already been written."

The three major problems of man are: Money, Relationship and Health. Interestingly, the solutions to these three major problems are found on the pages of books. He who cultivates the habit of having regular intercourse with great minds will be blessed with money, good relationship and sound health.

Books and ideas

It is a fact that ideas rule the world. Napoleon Hill in his book "Think and grow rich" said all we need for financial breakthrough is just one idea. That is absolutely correct and the good news is *"books are the surest, guaranteed source of ideas"*.

Men of the past who have accomplished worthwhile goals in every field of endeavors have poured out their souls, they have documented their thoughts and ideas in books, periodical, magazines and journals. All we have to do to be partakers of these great opportunities is to rub our minds with their superior minds.

William Ellery Channing had a spiritual insight and great understanding of this fact and he stated it in the following piece:

"It is chiefly through books that we enjoy intercourse with superior minds. In the best books, great men talk to us, give us their most precious thoughts, and pour their souls into ours. God be thanked for books. They are the voices of the distant and the dead, and make us heirs of the spiritual life of past ages. Books are true levelers. They give to all who will faithfully use them, the society, the spiritual presence, of the best and greatest of our race."

An Empire is born

We have all heard about the great empire called HSBC (Hong-Kong and Shangai Banking Corporation), one of the largest international banks on the high street founded in 1865 and still thriving today after 152 years.

What many of us do not know however was the fact that the idea behind the establishment of this great empire was given to a man – Thomas Sutherland while reading.

In 1864, while on a voyage by the SS Manila between Hong Kong and Foochow, Sutherland came across an article in a twenty-year old edition of Blackwood's Magazine on the advantages of Scottish banking. On the basis of this he concluded that founding a bank on Scottish principles would not be difficult. Recalling this article and recognizing that the founding of a local bank had now become a matter of urgency, he decided to fill the want complained of; he would be the one to push the establishment of a local bank.

(Biographies of Scotsmen)

Read and grow rich

Do you desire to be wealthy? Begin at once to have intercourse with superior minds on daily basis. This habits nurture ambition and keeps desire for a prosperous life alive. Money flows in the direction of a man or woman who is ready for it.

Reading good books prepares our minds and gets us ready for opportunities. If you cultivate the habit of reading and constantly thinking and digesting the information obtained from the pages of those books, your financial position will improve drastically. That is guaranteed, just give it a trial.

Brian Tracy, the celebrated author of "Getting Rich your own way" acknowledged he became a millionaire starting from nothing by having intercourse with the minds of great authors. One of such great authors was Napoleon Hill. From the pages of those prints Brian came across life changing principles which he applied in his business. Today, money is not his problem.

What about Bob Proctor, the Chairman of Proctor Gallagher Institute? Bob said he has been having intercourse with the mind of Napoleon Hill for the past fifty years by studying his book "Think and grow Rich". Bob acknowledged this book practically made him a millionaire.

The whole career of Franklin took a new dive in the right direction and was greatly influenced when he began to have intercourse with the mind of Cotton Mather through his book "Essay to Do Good".

Most of us do not know who we really are or what we are called to be until we start going through the pages of those

"GOLDEN TREASURES" called BOOKS. Good books awaken ambition and bring to the surface slumbering possibilities. No one can truly estimate the real value of books.

That is the truth my friend. If you really want to be rich, if you want to prosper in your career or business, you must start from now to have regular intercourse with superior minds.

Reading versus Earning

An average CEO in America we are told regularly have intercourse with the minds of at least four to five authors every month. An average American on the other hand reads just one book a year. To make the situation worse, sixty percent of those average Americans that read just one book a year, we are told never get pass the first chapter.

If you think this information is not true, there is only one way to find out, ask yourself, "how many books you have read in the last 6 months". If your answer is "nothing", you are not on the right path, and you need to change your direction if you want to become rich.

Now, listen to this, according to the figures released in 2016 by the American Federation of Labor and Congress on Industrial Organizations (AFL - CIO), CEOs of S&P 500 index companies on the average earn 347 times the wages of production and non-supervisory workers in the year 2016.

That means assuming the average annual wage of a production and non-supervisory worker in 2016 was $15,000 (Fifteen thousand dollars), then an average CEO of S&P 500 index companies earned $5,205,000 (Five Million, Two hundred and five thousand dollars) in the same year.

Although, there has been a lot of criticism about this high level of inequalities in the pay ratio, the only point I am trying to make here is that the more you know, the more your earning power is likely to increase.

Books and divine approval

Many people, especially in the religious sector are constantly praying to God for one blessing or the other and they fail to receive because they neglect the instruction to read. The blessings for which they seek are boldly provided on the pages of books.

It is for the benefits of these set of people that the bible clearly provides the following instruction in the book of Timothy:

Study to show thyself approved unto God, a workman that needs not be ashamed, rightly dividing the word of truth.

Books are clearly a means to receiving God's divine approval.

PART FOUR

Books And Mind Development

Chapter 4

Mind Development Through Reading

One of the most important things that wise men get out of their schooldays is a familiarity with books in various departments of learning. The ability to pick out from a library what will be most helpful in life is of the greatest value. It is like a man selecting his tools for intellectual expansion and social service.

Libraries are no longer a luxury, but a necessity. A home without books is like a house without windows. Children learn to read by being in the midst of books; they unconsciously absorb knowledge by handling them. No family can now afford to be without good reading.

It is reported that Henry Clay's mother furnished him with books by her own earnings at the washtub. Children who are well supplied with dictionaries, encyclopedias, histories, works of reference, and other useful books, will educate themselves unconsciously and almost without expense, and will learn many things of their own accord in moments which would otherwise be wasted in playing video games and watching televisions.

Besides, homes are brightened and made attractive by good books, and children stay in such pleasant homes; while those whose education has been neglected are anxious to get away from home, drift off, and fall into all manner of snares and dangers.

It is splendid for children to be brought up in the atmosphere of books, and it is astonishing how much a child will absorb from good books, if allowed to use them constantly, to handle them, to be familiar with their texts and titles.

How to profit from reading

Many people never make a mark on their books, they never underscore a choice passage. Their books are just as clean as the day they bought them, and often their minds are just about as clear of information.

Don't be afraid to mark your books. Make notes in them. They will be all the more valuable. One who learns to use his books in early life grows up with an increasing power for effective usefulness. Wear threadbare clothes and patched shoes, if necessary, but do not pinch or economize on books.

If you cannot afford to give your children luxurious gifts, you must place within their reach good books which will lift them above their surroundings, into respectability and honor. Everything is easier now as you can get some of these books free in the public libraries in your communities. But you still need to invest some dollars for books collection.

Each home is the place where children should get their early principal training for life. Parents should not be delusional thinking it is the responsibilities of teachers in the school. It is at home that children form habits which shape their careers, and which cling to them as long as they live. It is here at home that regular, persistent mental training will fix the life of the kids ever after.

Enabling environment for greatness

There are some pitiable homes today where ambitious boys and girls have longed to improve themselves, but were prevented from doing so by the negative habits prevailing in the home, where everybody else spent the evenings talking, joking, watching television and playing video games with no effort at self-improvement, no thought of higher ideals, no impulse to read anything better than a cheap, emotional stories.

Even sometimes, the aspiring members of the family who are eager to do something useful were teased and laughed at until they got discouraged and gave up the struggle. If some of the younger ones do not want to read or study themselves, they will not let anybody else who is so inclined do so.

Children are naturally mischievous, and like to tease. They are selfish, too, and cannot understand why anyone else should want to go off by himself to read or study when they want him to play.

The young people would look forward to the study hour with as much anticipation as to playing if parents provide the enabling environment. Providing enabling environment for study is a means to a child's greatness.

Sweet hour of study

There are parents who understand what life is all about and they ensure that everyone, the children, the father and mother, by mutual consent, set aside a portion of each evening for study or some form of self-culture.

After dinner, they give themselves completely to recreation. They have a regular romp and play, and all the fun possible for an hour. Then when the time comes for study, the entire house becomes so still that you could hear a pin drop. Everyone is in his place reading, writing, studying, or engaged in some form of mental work.

No one is allowed to speak or disturb anyone else. If any member of the family is indisposed, or for any reason does not feel like working, he must at least keep quiet and not disturb the others.

There is perfect harmony and unity of purpose — an ideal condition for study. Everything that would scatter the efforts or cause the mind to wander, all interruptions that would break the continuity of thought, are carefully guarded against. More is gained in one hour of close, uninterrupted study than in two or three broken by many interruptions, or weakened by mind wandering.

If it were possible for every family that squanders precious time to spend one evening in such a home, it would be an inspiration. A bright, intelligent, harmonious atmosphere surround a self-improving home that one feels insensibly uplifted and stimulated to better things.

Sometimes the habits of a home are revolutionized by the influence of one determined youth who declares himself, taking a stand and announcing that, as for himself, he does not intend to be a failure, that he is going to take no chances as to his future.

The moment he does this, he stands out in strong contrast with the great mass of young people who are throwing away their opportunities and have not grit and stamina enough to do anything worthwhile.

Your very reputation of always trying to improve yourself in every possible way, of being dead in earnest, will attract the attention of everybody who knows you, and you will get many recommendations for promotion and unusual opportunities which never comes to those who make no special effort to climb upward.

The generation of time wasters

There is a great deal of time wasted even in the busiest lives, which, if properly organized, might be used to advantage. Many housewives who are so busy from morning to night that they really believe they have no time for reading books, would be amazed to find how much they would have if they would more thoroughly organize their work.

Order is a great time saver, and we certainly ought to be able to adjust our living plan that we can have a fair amount of time for self-improvement, for enlarging our lives. Yet many people think that their only opportunity for self-improvement depends upon the time left after everything else has been attended to.

What would a business man accomplish if he did not attend to important matters until he had time that was not needed for anything else? The good business man goes to his office in the morning and plunges right into the important work of the day.

He knows perfectly well that if he attends to all the outside matters, all the details and little things that come up, sees everybody that wants to see him, and answers all the questions people want to ask, it will be time to close his office before he gets to his main business.

Where there is a will, there is always a way

Most of us manage somehow to find time for the things we love. If one is hungry for knowledge, if one yearns for self-improvement, if one has a taste for reading, he will make the opportunity. Where the heart is, there is the treasure. Where the ambition is, there is time.

It takes not only resolution but also determination to set aside non essentials for the essentials. There is always the temptation to sacrifice future good for present pleasure; to put off reading to a more convenient season, while we enjoy idle amusements or waste the time in gossip or frivolous conversation.

The greatest things of the world have been done by those who systematized their work and organized their time. Men who have left their mark on the world have appreciated the preciousness of time, regarding it as their greatest asset. If you want to develop a delightful form of enjoyment, to cultivate a new pleasure, a new sensation which you have never before experienced, begin at once to read good books regularly every day.

Do not stress out yourself by trying to read a great deal at first. Read a little at a time, but read some portion every day, no matter how little. If you are faithful you will soon acquire a taste for reading and your reading habit will improve drastically, and it will, in time, give you infinite satisfaction, and unalloyed pleasure.

3 and 3 formula for Reading

In my other books, I teach people the easiest way to start the habit of reading. This formula makes it easy, realizing you don't have to read a lot at a time when you are just starting out. The formula is to read three pages in the morning before you start you daily activities and also read three pages at night before you go to bed at night.

It only takes around fifteen minutes to read three pages at a time. I believe thirty minutes a day is not too much for your self-development if you are really serious about it. Following this formula means you will read six pages a day, forty-two pages a week and one hundred and sixty-eight pages in a month.

That is approximately 2 books at the end of each month if you start with books with about seventy-five to eighty pages. I recommend you start with books with less than hundred pages at first. You may then proceed with books with more pages once you have formed the habit. It is easier to stick to the habit if you start with short books than if you start with long books with many pages which you may not finish before you get bored and give up.

If you continue with this formula, you would have read about twenty-four books at the end of the year. This is like becoming a Ph.D. holder in your field. Your life will be completely transformed to your own amazement. Give it a trial, you have nothing to lose.

The Power of organization and focus in Reading

In a physical training room, one often sees people, who, instead of pursuing a systematic course of training to develop all the muscles of the body, flit aimlessly from one thing to another, exercising with pulley-weights for a minute or two, walking on the treadmill for another 2 minutes and, swinging once or twice on parallel bars, and so frittering away time and strength.

It is perhaps far better for such people to stay away from a gymnasium altogether, for their lack of purpose and continuity makes them lose rather than gain muscular energy. A man or woman who would gather strength from gymnastic exercise must set about it systematically and with a will. He must put mind and energy into the work, or else continue to have flabby muscles and an undeveloped body.

There is a great similarity between the physical gymnasium and mental exercise. Thoroughness and system are as necessary in one as in the other. It is not the tasters of books, not those who sample here and there, who take up one book after another, turn the leaves listlessly and hurry to the end, who strengthen and develop the mind by reading.

To get the most from your reading you must read with a purpose. To sit down and pick up a book listlessly, with no aim except to pass away time, is demoralizing. It is much as if an employer were to hire a boy, and tell him he could start when he pleased in the morning, work when he felt like it, rest when he wanted to, and quit when he got tired.

Never go to a book you wish to read for a particular purpose with a tired, stressed mentality. If you do, you will derive nothing from it. Go to it fresh, vigorous, and with active, never passive, faculties. This practice is a splendid and effective cure for mind-wandering, which afflicts so many people.

Nothing can give greater satisfaction than reading with a purpose. The consciousness of a broadening mind that follows reading; the consciousness that we are pushing ignorance, bigotry, and whatever clouds the mind and hampers progress a little further away from us is life transforming.

The kind of reading that counts, that builds mental fiber and stamina, is that upon which the mind is concentrated. We should approach a book with our mind and soul concentrating upon its contents. Passive reading is even more harmful in its effects than desultory reading. It will not strengthen the brain any more than sitting in a gymnasium will develop the body.

The mind remains inactive, in a sort of indolent manner, wandering here and there, without focusing anywhere. Such reading sucks out mental energies, weakens the intellect, and makes the brain lethargic and incapable of grappling with great principles and difficult problems.

What you get out of a book is not necessarily what the author puts into it, but what you bring to it. If the mind does not lead the head, if the thirst for knowledge, the hunger for a broader and deeper culture, are not the motives for reading, you will not get the most out of a book.

But, if your thirsty soul drinks in the writer's thought as the dry soil absorbs rain, then your latent possibilities and the potency of your being, like seeds in the soil, will spring forth into new life. Your entire life will have new meaning when you read as Macaulay did, as Carlyle did, as Lincoln did — as did all great men who have profited by their reading, with your whole soul absorbed in what you are reading, with such intense concentration that you will be oblivious of everything else outside of your book.

Reading Versus Thinking

Reading furnishes us only with the materials of knowledge," said John Locke, " it is thinking that makes what we read ours." In order to get the most out of books, the reader must be a thinker. The mere acquisition of facts is not the acquisition of power.

Napoleon Hill in his popular book "Think and Grow Rich" said:

"It is lack of understanding of this fact that has been the source of confusion to millions of people who falsely believe that knowledge is power. He said it is nothing of the sort. Knowledge is only potential power. It becomes power only when, and if, it is organized into definite plans of action and directed to a definite end.

To fill the mind with all sort of knowledge that cannot be practically organized into a useful purpose is like filling our houses with furniture and various articles until we have no room to move about. Food does not become physical force, brain, or muscle until it has been thoroughly digested and assimilated, and has become an integral part of the blood, brain, and other tissues.

Knowledge does not become power until it has been digested and assimilated by the brain, until it has become a part of the mind itself. If you wish to become intellectually strong, after reading with the closest attention, form this habit: frequently close your book and sit and think, or stand and walk and think, but think, contemplate, and reflect.

Turn what you have read over and over in your mind. It is not yours until you have assimilated it by your thought and taken it into your life. When you first read it, it belongs to the author. It is yours only when it becomes an integral part of you.

Many people have an idea that if they keep reading everlastingly, if they have a book in their hands during every leisure moment, they will, of necessity, become full-rounded and well-educated. This is a mistake. They might just as well expect to become athletes by eating at every opportunity.

It is not the number of books," says Professor William Mathews, which a young man reads that makes him intelligent and well informed, but the number of well-chosen ones that he has mastered, so that every valuable thought in them is a familiar friend.

It is even more necessary to think than to read. Thinking, contemplating what we have read, is what digestion and assimilation are to the food. Some of the people who appear to be reading are always cramming themselves with knowledge. They are everlastingly reading, but they never think.

When they get a few minutes of spare time, they snatch a book and go to read. In other word, they are always eating intellectually, but never digest their knowledge or assimilate it.

You should bring your mind to the reading of a book, or to the study of any subject, as you take an axe to the grindstone; not for what you get from the stone, but for the sharpening of the axe. The greatest advantage of books does not always come under what we remember of them, but from their suggestiveness, their character-building power.

It is a grand thing to read a good book, but it is grander to live a good life — and in the living of such life is generated the power that defies age and its decadence. It is not the ability, the education, the knowledge that one has that makes the difference between men.

The mere possession of knowledge is not always the possession of power; knowledge, which has not become a part of yourself, knowledge which cannot swing into line in an emergency is of little use, and will not save you at the critical moment.

The effective man

To be effective, a man's education must become a part of him as he goes along. All of it must be worked up into power. A little practical education that has become a part of one's being and is always available, will accomplish more in the world than knowledge far more extensive that cannot be utilized.

No one better illustrates what books will do for a man, and what a thinker will do with his books, than Gladstone, who was always far greater than his career. He rose above Parliament, reached out beyond politics, and was always growing.

He had a passion for intellectual expansion. His peculiar gifts undoubtedly fitted him for the church, or he would have made a good professor at Oxford or Cambridge, but circumstances led him into the political arena, and he adapted himself readily to his environment.

He was an all-round, well-read man, who thought his way through libraries and through life. One great benefit of a taste for reading and access to the book world, is the service it renders as a diversion and a solace. What a great thing to be able to get away from ourselves, to fly away from the harassing, humiliating, discouraging, depressing things about us, to go at will to a world of beauty, joy, and gladness.

If a person is discouraged or depressed by any great bereavement or suffering, the quickest and the most effective way of restoring the mind to its perfect balance, to its normal condition, is to immerse it in a sane atmosphere, an uplifting, encouraging, inspiring atmosphere, and this may always be readily found in the best books.

The Uplifting power of books

From any work, the man with a happy taste for books comes in tired and falls into the arms of some great author, who raises him from the ground and takes him into a new heaven and a new earth, where he forgets his bruises and rests his limbs, and he returns to the world a fresh and happy man. No one can overestimate the value of good books.

In good books, the finest minds give us the best wisdom of present and past ages; the intellects gifted far beyond ours, are ready to give us the results of lifetimes of patient thought, imaginations open to the beauty of the universe.

The lover of good books can never be lonely; and, no matter where he is, he will always find pleasant and profitable occupation and the best of society when he quits work. Who can ever be grateful enough for the art of printing, grateful enough to the famous authors who have put their best thoughts where we can enjoy them at will?

There are many advantages of having intercourse with great minds through their books over meeting them in person. The best of them lives in their books, while their disagreeable peculiarities, their idiosyncrasies, their objectionable traits are eliminated.

In their books we find the authors at their best. Their thoughts are selected, winnowed in their books. Books are friends and are always at our service. No matter how nervous, tired, or discouraged we may be, they are always soothing, stimulating and uplifting.

Free uninterrupted access to the best celebrities

We may call up the greatest writer in the middle of the night when we cannot sleep, and he is just as glad to be with us as at any other time. We are not excluded from any nook or cranny of the great literary world.

We can visit the most celebrated people that ever lived without an appointment, without influence, without the necessity of dressing or of observing any rules of etiquette. We can drop in upon Lincoln, Washington, Milton, Shakespeare, Emerson, Longfellow, Carnegie, Rockefeller, without a moment's notice and receive the warmest welcome.

You get the attention of the best of the best in our great libraries, with the huge advantage of needing no introduction, and not dreading repulses. From that great crowd of celebrities, you can choose the companion that pleases you. For in the silent auditorium of the immortals there is no pride, but the highest is at the service of the lowest, with a grand humility.

You may speak freely with the best, without a thought of your inferiority, for books are perfectly well bred, and hurt no one's feelings by any discriminations.

Repetition provides free access into the holy of holies

It is only when books have been read and re-read with ever deepening delight that they are clasped to the heart, and become what Macaulay found them to be, the old friends who are never found with new faces, who are the same to us in our wealth and in our poverty, in our glory and in our obscurity.

No one gets into the innermost heart of a beautiful poem, a great history, a book of delicate humor, or a volume of exquisite essays, by reading it once or twice. He must have its precious thoughts and illustrations stored in the treasure-house of memory, and brood over them in the hours of leisure.

A book may be a perpetual companion. Friends come and go, but the book may beguile all experiences and enchant all hours. The first time, says Goldsmith, "that I read an excellent book, it is to me just as if I had gained a new friend, when I read over a book I have perused before, it resembles the meeting with an old one.

A book is good company, said Henry Ward Beecher. It comes to your longing with full instruction, but pursues you never. It is not offended at your absent-mindedness, nor jealous if you turn to other pleasures of dress, or mineral, or even other books. It silently serves the soul of those who seek solace in it until they have been placed on thrones to dine with kings.

PART FIVE

Books And Leadership

Chapter 5

SELF-IMPROVEMENT,
the sure path to leadership

Gascoigne in his wisdom said *"A boy is better unborn than untaught"*.

When education has been neglected, either by reason of lack of opportunity, or because advantage was not taken of the opportunities afforded, the one remaining hope is self-improvement.

Books, our greatest assets in the 21st century

Opportunities for self-improvement surround us, the helps- to self-improvement are abundant, and in this day of cheap books, free libraries, and evening schools, there can be no good excuse for neglect to use the faculties for mental growth and development which are so abundantly supplied.

When we look at the difficulties which hindered the acquisition of knowledge ages ago; the scarcity and the costliness of books, the value of the dimmest candle light, the unremitting toil which left so little time for study, the physical weariness which had to be overcome to enable mental exertion in study, we may well marvel at the giants of scholarship those days of hardship produced.

And when we add to these limitations physical disabilities, blindness, deformity, ill-health, which many contended against, we may feel ashamed as we contemplate the fullness of modern opportunity and the helps and incentives to study self-development which are so lavishly provided for our use and inspiration, and of which we avail ourselves so little.

Golden treasures in spare moments

Self-improvement implies one essential feeling: the desire for improvement. If the desire exists, then improvement is usually accomplished only by the conquest of self, the material self, which seeks pleasure and amusement. It is this type of self-discipline that will ensure desired results.

For all who seek self-improvement, " there is a lion in the way," the lion of self-indulgence, and it is only by the conquest of this enemy that progress is assured. Show me how a youth spends his evenings, his odd bits of time, and I will forecast his future.

Does he look upon this leisure as precious, rich in possibilities, as containing golden material for his future life structure? Or does he look upon it as an opportunity for self-indulgence, for a light, flippant "good time "?

The way he spends his leisure will give the keynote of his life, will tell whether he is dead in earnest, or whether he looks upon life as a joke. He may not be conscious of the terrible effect, the gradual deterioration of character which comes from a frivolous wasting of his evenings and half-holidays, but the character is being undermined just the same.

Young men are often surprised to find themselves dropping behind their competitors, but if they will examine themselves, they will find that they have stopped growing because they have ceased their effort to keep abreast of time, to be widely read, to enrich their life with self-culture.

The right use of spare moments in reading and study is an indication of superior qualities. And in many historic cases the " spare " moments utilized for study were not spare in the sense of being the spare time of leisure. They were rather spared moments, moments spared from sleep, from meal times, from recreation.

A leader in the Blacksmith shop

Where is the boy who has less chance to rise in the world than Elihu Burritt, apprenticed at sixteen to a blacksmith, in whose shop he had to work at the forge all the day light, and often by candle light? Yet he managed, by studying with a book before him at his meals, carrying it in his pocket that he might utilize every spare moment, and studying at night and on holidays, to pick up an excellent education in the odds and ends of time which most boys throw away.

While the rich boy and the idler were yawning and stretching and getting their eyes open, young Burritt had seized the opportunity and improved it. He had a thirst for knowledge and a desire for self-improvement, which overcame every obstacle in his pathway. A wealthy gentleman offered to pay his expenses at Harvard, but Elihu said he could get his education himself, even though he had to work twelve or fourteen hours a day at the forge.

Here was a determined boy. He snatched every spare moment at the anvil and forge as if it were gold. He believed, with Gladstone, that thrift of time would repay him in after years with usury, and that waste of it would make him dwindle. Think of a boy working nearly all the daylight in a blacksmith shop, and yet finding time to study seven languages in a single year.

Why many remain followers all their life

It is not lack of ability that holds men down and forever keeps them on the treadmill, going nowhere but lack of industry. In many cases the employees have better brains, better mental capacities than their employers. But they do not improve their faculties. They dull their mind by vicious habits.

They spend their time and money at the pool table and in the pub and as they grow old, and the harness of perpetual service gall them, they grumble at their lack of luck, their limited opportunities. These kind of employees remain perpetual clerks and rotten away in the job they do not like because they did not think it worthwhile as boys and girls to learn to write a good hand or to master the fundamental branches of knowledge requisite in a business career.

The ignorance common among young men and young women in factories, stores, and offices, everywhere, in fact, in this age of opportunities where youth could be well educated, and become a leader is a pitiable thing. In every angle, we see men and women of natural abilities occupying inferior positions because they did not think it of enough importance in their youth to concentrate their attention on the acquisition of knowledge that would make them proficient workers.

They find themselves held back, handicapped for life, because of the seeming trifles which they did not think it worthwhile to pay attention to in their youth. Many a girl of good natural ability spends her most productive years as a cheap clerk or in a mediocre position because she never thought it worthwhile to develop her mental faculties or to take advantage of opportunities within reach to fit herself for a superior position.

She did not think it would pay to go to the bottom of any study at school, to learn to keep accounts accurately, or fit herself to do anything in such a way as to be able to make a living by it. She expected to marry and depend on her husband, and never prepared for being dependent on herself, — a contingency against which marriage, in many instances, is no safeguard.

Leadership - a function of hours of intercourse with superior minds

The trouble with most youths is that they are not willing to fling the whole weight of their being into their vocation. They want short hours, little work and a lot of play. They think more of leisure and pleasure than of discipline and training in their great life specialty.

Many a clerk envies his employer and wishes that he could go into business for himself and be an employer also, but he thinks it is too much work to make the effort to rise above a clerk position. He likes to take life easy; and he wonders idly whether, after all, it is worthwhile to strain and strive and struggle and study to prepare oneself for the sake of getting up a little higher and making a little more money.

The trouble with a great many people is that they are not willing to make present sacrifices for future gain. They prefer to have a good time as they go along, rather than spend time in self-improvement. They have a vague wish to do something great, but few have that intensity of longing which impels them to make the sacrifice of the present for the future.

Few are willing to work underground for years laying a foundation for their life structure. They yearn for greatness, but their yearning is not the kind which is willing to pay any price or make any sacrifice for its object. So the majority slide along in mediocrity all their lives.

They have ability for something higher up, but they have not the energy and determination to prepare for it. They do not care to make the necessary effort. They prefer to take life easier and lower down rather than to struggle for something higher. They do not play the game for all they are worth. If a man has but the disposition for self-improvement and advancement he will find opportunity to rise to the position of leadership, or what he cannot find, he will create.

A leader aboard the man-of-war

Here is an example from the everyday life going on around us and in which we are all taking part. A young Irishman who had reached the age of nineteen or twenty without learning to read or write, left home because of the intemperance that prevailed there, learned to read a little by studying billboards, and eventually got a position as steward aboard a man-of-war. He chose that occupation and got leave to serve at the captain's table because of a great desire to learn.

He kept a little tablet in his coat-pocket, and whenever he heard a new word wrote it down. One day an officer saw him writing and immediately suspected him of being a spy. When he and the other officers learned what the tablet was used for, the young man was given more opportunities to learn, and these led in time to promotion, until, finally, he won a prominent position in the navy. Success as a naval officer prepared the way for success in other fields.

Self-improvement has accomplished about all the great things of the world. How many young men falter, faint, and dally with their purpose, because they have no capital to start with, and wait and wait for some good luck to give them a lift. But success is the child of hard work and perseverance. It cannot be coaxed or bribed; pay the price and it is yours.

The greatest regret in the world

One of the sad things about the neglected opportunities for self-improvement is that they put people of great natural ability at a disadvantage among those who are their mental inferiors.

One of the most humiliating experiences that can ever come to a human being is to be conscious of possessing more than ordinary ability, and yet be tied to an inferior position because of lack of early and intelligent training commensurate with this ability.

To know that one has ability to realize eighty or ninety per cent of his possibilities, but because of the lack of proper education and training, to be unable to bring out more than twenty-five per cent of it, is humiliating.

In other words, to go through life conscious that you are making a botch of your capabilities just because of lack of training, is a most depressing, mortifying thing. Nothing else outside of sin causes more sorrow than that which comes from not having prepared for the highest career possible to one.

There are no more bitter regrets than those which result from being obliged to let pass opportunities for which one never prepared himself.

I read a pitiable case of a born naturalist whose ambition was so suppressed and whose education so neglected in youth that later, when he came to know more about natural history than almost any man of his day, he could not write a grammatical sentence, and could never make his ideas live in words, perpetuate them in books, because of his ignorance of even the rudiments of an education.

His early vocabulary was so narrow and pinched, and his knowledge of his language so limited, that he always seemed to be painfully struggling for words to express his thought. Think of the suffering of this splendid man, who was conscious of possessing colossal scientific knowledge, and yet was absolutely unable to express himself grammatically.

Make hay while the sun shines

While it is true that age is never a barrier to self-development, it is always better to begin this process very early in life when there is boundless energy, unquenchable drive, unlimited enthusiasm and everlasting ambition. All these impetuses that add fire to a man's bones decline with age.

I always feel sorry for such people who have passed the school age and who will probably go through life with their splendid minds handicapped by ignorance which, even late in life, they might largely or entirely overcome. It is such a pity that a young man, for instance, who has the natural ability which would make him a leader among men, must, for the lack of a little training and preparation, work for somebody else, perhaps with scarcely half of his ability.

Everywhere we see clerks, mechanics, employees in all walks of life, who cannot rise to anything like positions which correspond with their natural ability, because they have not had the education. They are ignorant. They cannot write an intelligent letter. They murder the English language, and hence their superb ability cannot be demonstrated, and remains in mediocrity.

The parable of the talents illustrates and enforces one of nature's sternest laws: " *To him that hath shall be given; from him that hath not shall be taken away even that which he hath.*" Scientists call this law the survival of the fittest.

The fittest are those who use what they have, who gain strength by struggle, and who survive by self-development through control of their hostile or helpful environment. The soil, the sunshine, and the atmosphere are very liberal with the material for the growth of the plant or the tree, but the plant must use all it gets, must work it up into flowers, into fruit, into leaf or fiber or something, or the supply will cease.

In other words, the soil will not send any more building material up the sap than is used for growth, and the faster this material is used the more rapid the growth, the more abundantly the material will come. The same law holds good everywhere.

Swim or Sink in nature's unrestricted resources

Nature is liberal with us if we utilize what she gives us, but if we stop using it, if we do not do some building somewhere, if we do not transform the material which she gives us into force and utilize that force, we not only find the supply cut off, but also that we are growing weaker, and less efficient.

Everything in nature is on the move, either one way or the other. It is either going up or down. It is either advancing or retrograding; we cannot hold without using. Nature withdraws muscle or brain if we do not use them. She withdraws skill the moment we stop using it efficiently.

The force is withdrawn when we cease exercising it. A college graduate is often surprised years after he leaves his college to find that about all he has to show for his education is his diploma. The power and efficiency which he gained there have been lost because he has not been using them.

He thought at the time when everything was still fresh in his mind, after his examination, that this knowledge would remain with him forever, but it has been slipping away from him every minute since he stopped using it. The only that has remained and increased is the little which he has used. The rest has evaporated away.

A great many college men ten years after graduation find that they have but very little to show for their four years' course, because they have not utilized their knowledge. They have become weaklings without knowing it. They constantly say to themselves, I have a college education, I must have some ability, I must amount to something in the world.

But the college diploma has no more power to hold the knowledge you have gained in college than a piece of tissue paper over a gas jet can hold the gas in the pipe. Everything which you do not use is constantly slipping away from you. Use it or lose it. The secret of power is use. Ability will not remain with us; force will evaporate the moment we cease to do something with it.

The tools for self-improvement are in your hands, use them properly and you will find yourself in the position of leadership. If the axe is dull, then more strength must be put forth to get it sharpened. If your opportunities are limited because your mind has become dull for lack of use, you must put more energy, put forth more effort. Progress may seem slow at first, but perseverance assures success. Line upon line, and precept upon precept is the rule of mental up-building, and in due time ye shall reap if ye faint not."

Leaders are readers

It is a great fact that leaders are readers. Take a look at every field, every walks of life and you will find out for yourself that the leaders at the top of these various fields are good readers. This will renew hope in you that your destiny is in your own hand and you are not a product of any unfortunate environment. If you want to make any impact in life, all you have to do is take to books and begin to have intercourse with superior minds. Let us take a look at the following fields:

Medicine

Professor Ben Carson is my hero. His life had a very great influence on me developing the habit of reading. He is a very highly revered figure in the medical field. He attributed his success in life to his love of reading.

In his own words, Dr. Carson said:

My mother made me and my brother watch a small amount of television and made us read books. In the course of reading those books, he continues, I read about a lot of people, successful people, and I come to realize that the person who has the most to do with what happen to you in life is you.

Not somebody else, not some outside influence, or some environmental factors, it is you and the choices you make. Once I realized that, poverty didn't bother me anymore because I know I can change that.

In 1987, the medical profession recorded an outstanding breakthrough and Dr. Carson became the first neurosurgeon to successfully separate Siamese twins joined at the back of the head (occipital craniopagus). When asked how this was accomplished, he attributed it to bringing together piece by piece all the information he had acquired from his reading and interactions with other colleagues.

Personal development

Bob Proctor and Brian Tracy who are my great mentors are advocates of reading. No wonder they are great leaders in the personal development industry. Both of them practically acknowledged, the book "Think and grow Rich" by Napoleon Hill made them millionaires.

Bob told us he recently built a library in his home and position himself in the middle of it because he wants to be surrounded with the minds of the greatest in human history. Brian who has authored so many books himself gave an account of how much he values reading. I am very fascinated with the lives of these men, how they are still very active and strong at the age where so many would have retired.

Religion, Politics, and Business

Suppose you have the opportunity to be invited into the homes of great spiritual leaders, homes of W.F Kumuyi, the general superintendent of the Deeper Christian life Ministry, E.A Adeboye, the general overseer of the Redeemed Christian Church of God, Bishop D. Oyedepo, the Bishop of winners Chapel.

Suppose you have the rare privilege to be invited into the homes of great leaders in politics, homes of George Washington, Abraham Lincoln and J.F Kennedy - the first, sixteenth and thirty fifth Presidents of the United States respectively.

Assuming you are given the golden privilege to take a tour through the homes of great minds in the world of business, through the homes of people like Steve Jobs of Apple, Richard Branson of Virgin, Jeff Bezos of Amazon.

Even though these people are from different walks of life, different countries and different ethnic backgrounds, what is that one single thing you think will be common to those homes?

If you guess right, it will be that the homes of these people have a library in them. Do you think that happens by accident or you think it is just a matter of coincidence? No, it is not. Leaders are readers. Charlie Tremendous Jones said:

"You are today what you will be five years from now, except for the books you read and the people you associate with.

PART SIX

Books And Character Development

Chapter 6

Develop a pleasing Personality through reading

Perhaps there is nothing else which enters more deeply into the very core of one's character than the books one reads. One of the greatest blessings that can come to a young life is the love of good books.

The practice of keeping before the young, growing mind beautiful and uplifting images, bright, cheerful, healthy thoughts from good books, is of inestimable value. The difference between the future of the boy who has formed the habit of good reading and the one who has not is as great as that between the educated and the uneducated youth.

Next to the actual society of a noble, high-minded author is the benefit to be gained by reading his books. The mind is brought into harmony with the hopes, the aspirations, the ideals of the writer, so that it is impossible, afterwards, to be satisfied with low or ignoble things.

The horizon of the reader broadens, his point of view changes, his ideals are higher and nobler, his whole outlook on life is more elevated. The importance of having great models, high ideals, held constantly before the mind when it is in a plastic condition, cannot be overestimated.

The books we read in youth may make or mar our lives. Many a man has attributed his first start and all his after success to the books read in his boyhood. They opened up to him his possibilities, indicated his tastes, his tendencies, and helped him to find his place in life. They permit men and women to form examples that are useful in carrying out high ideals, and they bring pleasure and contentment to all.

Concentration and personal enlargement through reading

The habit of holding the mind steadily and persistently to the thought in a good book not only increases the power of concentration, but also improves the quality of the mind. It is not so much what we carry away from the book in the memory that is valuable, as the strength, stamina, and skill we develop in reading it.

The mind grows only when actively engaged, and it grows most rapidly when stretching itself to the utmost, not over straining, which is as fatal in the mental as in the physical gymnasium. Effective reading, therefore, is effective mind growth, mind enlargement, and to promote this, we must bring all of our power to bear on whatever we read.

We must approach a book with vigor, will, and determination, and with an undivided mind, or we shall absorb nothing of value. Inspiring reading is that in which life-building words abound, for words are things which unconsciously enrich character. The image of each helpful word held in the mind leaves its impress, its autograph, so to speak, there, and continually reproduces itself in uplifting thoughts.

If our homes were furnished with more character building books and less of television or destructive movies, our children would get a much better start in life. To bring a child up in an atmosphere of books, to surround him with the works of great minds from his infancy, and lead him gradually to an appreciation of the works of the intellectual giants of the race is equal to a liberal education.

The boy or girl so nurtured will have been given the best means of acquiring a mentality of the very highest order. Bacon said:

If I might control the literature of the household, I would guarantee the well-being of the church and the state.

The Value of a good book price $2 is more than a million dollar

It is impossible to estimate the value of the influence of any book upon a life, when we consider that many careers have turned upon the pivot of a single volume. In hundreds of instances, the future success of a boy has been traced to some book which inspired him.

A single book has often aroused a dormant ambition, awakened love for knowledge, and yearning for growth, and has sent a youth on the road of discovery.

It has led to important inventions, and has often supported and buttressed a young life against the floods of a sea of vice. How many there are who have been very successful in saving money, but whose minds are as barren of anything beautiful as is the hot sand of the Sahara Desert. These people are always ready to invest in land, stocks, or houses, but are never able to buy books or collect a library.

We know men who started out as bright, cheerful boys, with broad, generous minds, who have become so wedded to money-making, so absorbed in their business, that they cannot find time for anything else. They never travel or visit their friends.

They consider it foolish or extravagant to go to the opera or a good play. The daily paper limits the extent of their reading and recreation of any kind is relegated to a far-away future. Yet these people are surprised, when they retire from business late in life, to find that they have nothing to retire to, that they have destroyed the capacity for appreciating the things they thought they would enjoy.

Sweet or Bitter Personality

There are some people who, like the bee, gather honey from every flower, extracting sweetness even from a thistle, while others seem to distil bitterness from a clover blossom, a lily, or a rose. The difference between men lies in their early training or their habitual attitude of mind.

A life that has been rightly trained will extract sweetness from everything, it will see beauty in all things. There are superb personalities that go through life extracting sunshine from what to others seems but darkness, seeing charm in apparent ugliness, discerning grace and exquisite proportions where the unloving see but forbidding angles and distortion, and glimpsing the image of divinity where less beautiful souls see but a lost and degraded human being.

Yet it is a heritage possible to everyone who will take the trouble to begin early in life to cultivate the finer qualities of the soul. A beautiful character will make poetry out of the prosiest life, bring sunshine into the darkest home, and develop beauty and grace amid the ugliest surroundings.

It is not circumstances so much as the attitude and quality of the mind that give happiness, contentment, and divinity of service. It is a powerful aid toward the preservation and attainment of one's ideal in life to read, even if but a few moments each day, from great life-books which have helped so many souls, even in the midst of stumbling blocks, to build up beautiful characters.

Even the busiest man or woman can find a little time to get a daily glimpse at some inspiring books. The mind is like a musical instrument, a violin, for instance, which, no matter how excellent it may be, requires to be put into tune every day, that it may conform with the laws of harmony.

So the mind must be attuned each day to high standards, so that there shall be no discord between it and the great model instrument, truth itself. Mere wealth can never be compared with an elevated, expanded, and growing mind. Money, with a narrow mental horizon, with a scarred and rutty life, can never for one moment compare with the satisfaction of living in or being in touch with the world in all its great interests, and possessing a mind elevated by love of wisdom and high thoughts.

To have one's mentality stirred by the passion for expansion, to be lifted out of the narrow rut of ignorance and introduced to the greatest minds of all time, to come into real appreciation of art and nature, to feel the divine touch of science, to be brought into close relationship with the entire universe, to quench one's thirst at the fountain of perpetual truth, is to get a glimpse of the joys of life.

PART SEVEN

Prove All Books And Hold
Onto That Which Is Good

Chapter 7

Alexander Graham Bell on what to read

Alexander Graham Bell who invented the telephone was once asked - did everything you ever studied help you attain success?

On the contrary, he responded. I did not begin real study until I was sixteen. Until that time, my principal study was – Reading Novels.

But the novels did not help me in the least, for they did not give me an insight into real life. It is only those books that give one a grasp of practical affairs that are helpful.

To read novels continuously is like reading fairy stories or Arabian Night's tales. It is a butterfly existence, so long as it lasts, but some day, one is called to stern reality, UNPREPARED. Biographies or character making, inspirational and life shaping books are fundamental to maximum achievement and should be given priority.

Fifteen Minutes to Success

Cultivate the habit of reading something good for a minimum of fifteen minutes a day. Although, thirty minutes a day as discussed under the 3 and 3 formula will be better. Fifteen minutes a day will in twenty years make all the difference between a cultivated and an uncultivated mind, provided you read what is good. By the good, I mean the proved treasures of the world, the intellectual treasures of the world in history, science, self-help, and biography.

If you can only read a few, let them be books of highest character and established fame. Such books are easily found, even in small public libraries. It is a cardinal rule that if you do not like a book, do not read it. What another likes, you may not.

Like attracts like. Did you know that the thing you are looking for is looking for you; that is the very law of affinities to get together? If you are coarse in your tastes, vicious in your tendencies, you do not have to work very hard to find coarse, vicious books; they are seeking you by the very law of attraction. One's taste for reading is much like his taste for food.

Dull books are to be avoided altogether, as one refuses food disagreeable to him. To someone else the book may not be dull, nor the food disagreeable. Whole nations may eat cabbage, or stale fish, while I like neither. Ultimately, every reader must make his own selection, and find the book that finds him.

Choose Carefully- your life is shaped by the books you read

Books can be divided into sheep and goats. It is possible that the careers of the majority of criminals in our prisons today might have been vastly different if the characters of their reading when they were young had been uplifting, and wholesome, instead of degrading.

Christian Endeavor Clark saw a notice conspicuously posted in a large city which says: All boys should read the wonderful story of the desperado brothers of the Western plains, whose strange and thrilling adventures of successful robbery and murder have never before been equaled. This is priced five cents.

The next morning, Dr. Clark read in a newspaper of that city that seven boys had been arrested for burglary, and four stores broken into by the gang. One of the ringleaders was only ten years old. At their trial, it appeared that each had invested five cents in the story of border crime, Red-eyed Dick, the Terror of the Rockies, or some of such stories which has poisoned many a lad's lives.

A seductive, demoralizing book destroys the ambition unless for vicious living. All that was sweet, beautiful, and wholesome in the character before seems to vanish, and everything changes after the reading of a single bad book. It has aroused the appetite for more forbidden pleasures, until it chases out the desire for everything better, purer, healthier.

Mental dissipation from this exciting literature, often dripping with suggestiveness of impurity, giving a passport to the prohibited, is fatal to all soundness of mind.

The influence of a bad book

A lad once showed to another a book full of words and pictures of impurity. He only had it in his hands a few moments. Later in life he held high office in the church, and years afterward told a friend that he would have given half he possessed had he never seen that book.

Light, flashy stories, with no moral to them, seriously injured the mind of a brilliant young lady I once knew. Her brain became completely demoralized by constant mental dissipation. Familiarity with the bad ruins the taste for the good. Her ambition and ideas of life became completely changed.

Her only enjoyment was the excitement of her imagination through vicious, unhealthy literature. Nothing else will more quickly injure a good mind than familiarity with the frivolous, and the superficial. Even though they may not be actually vicious, the reading of books which are not true to life, which carry home no great lesson, teach no sane or healthful philosophy, but are merely written to excite the passions, to stimulate a morbid curiosity, will ruin the best of minds in a very short time.

It tends to destroy the ideals and to ruin the taste for all good reading. In our reading we can take in the poison which kills, or we can drink in encouragement and inspiration which bids us look up. The poison in some books is extremely dangerous, because so subtle; the evil is often painted to look like good.

Beware of books which, though they may not contain a single bad word, yet reek with immoral suggestions. The spirit which pervades a book, the subtle motive in the author's mind when he wrote it, has everything to do with its influence. Read books which make you look up, which inspire you to be a little bigger man or woman, to amount to a little more in the world.

Read books that make you think more of yourself and believe more in yourself and in others. Beware of books that shake your confidence in your fellow man. Read constructive books, books that are builders; avoid those that tear down. Beware of authors who sap your faith in men and your respect for womanhood, who shake your faith in the sanctity of the home and scoff at religion, who undermine sense of duty and moral obligation.

Show me your books and I will predict your future

The books which we handle most often and value the highest are great tell-tales of our tastes and our ambition. A stranger could write a pretty good biography of a man he had never seen by careful examination and analysis of his reading matter.

Read, read, read all you can. But never read a bad book or a poor book. Life is too short, time too precious, to spend it in reading anything but the best. Any book which takes away your desire for a better and nobler life is bad for you.

Many people still hold that it is a bad thing for the young to read works of fiction. They believe that young minds get a moral twist from reading that which they know is not true, the descriptions of mere imaginary heroes and heroines, and of things which never happened.

Now, this is a very narrow, limited view of a big question. These people do not understand the office of the imagination; they do not realize that many of the fictitious heroes and heroines that live in our minds, even from childhood's days, are much more real in their influence on our lives than some of those that exist in flesh and blood.

Fiction books, if it is good and elevating, is a splendid exercise of all the mental and moral faculties, it increases courage, it arouses enthusiasm, it sweeps the brain-ash off the mind, and actually strengthens its ability to grasp new principles.

The reading of good fiction is a splendid imagination exerciser and builder. It stimulates imagination by suggestions, powerfully increases its picturing capacity, and keeps it fresh, vigorous, and wholesome. And a wholesome imagination plays a very great part in every sane and worthy life.

It makes it possible for us to shut out the most disagreeable past, to shut out at will all hideous memories of our mistakes, failures, and misfortunes.

It helps us to forget our trouble and sorrows, and to slip at will into a new, fresh world of our own making, a world which we can make as beautiful, as sublime, as we wish.

A well-developed imagination is a priceless asset

The imagination is a wonderful substitute for wealth, luxuries, and for material things. No matter how poor we may currently be, or how unfortunate our background, we can by its aid travel round the world, visit the greatest cities, and create the most beautiful things for ourselves.

A lad of fifteen bent over a borrowed volume of sea tales. For hours he reads on, oblivious of all surroundings, until parental attention is drawn toward him by the unusual silence. The boy is seen to be trembling from head to foot with suppressed excitement.

A fatherly hand is laid upon the volume, closing it firmly, and the edict is spoken, no more novels for five years. And the lad goes off to bed, half glad, half grieved, wondering whether he has found fetters or achieved freedom. In truth he had received both, for that undiscriminating command forbade to him, during a formative period of his life, works which would have kindled his imagination, enriched his fancy, and heightened his power of expression.

But it also saved him from a possible descent to the inferno; it made heroes of history, not demigods of mythology, his companions, and reserved to mature years those excursions in the literature of the imagination which may lead a young man up to heaven or as easily drag him down to hell. There was never such a demand for fiction as now, and never larger opportunities for its usefulness.

Nothing has such an attraction for life as life. But what the heart craves is not life as it is. It is life as it ought to be. We want not the feeble but the forceful, not the commonplace but the transcendent. Nobody objects to the ' purpose novel ' except those who object to the purpose.

Dealing as it does, in the hands of a great master, with the grandest passions, the most tender emotions, the divinest hopes, it can portray all these spiritual forces in their majestic sweep and uplift. And as a matter of history, we have seen the novel achieve in a single generation the task at which the homily had labored ineffectively for a hundred years.

Realizing this, it is safe to say that there is not a theory of the philosopher, a hope of the reformer, or a prayer of the saint which does not eventually take form in a story.

Recommended Inspiration books

When and what you chose to read is of course your decision to make and no one has any right to enforce on you an opinion except for children who are to be wisely and jealously guided by their parents and teachers. Since we all come from different walk of life, what we read to build our professional capabilities will be a matter for each one of us to decide by exercising our good judgements.

However, we all need inspiration, motivation and encouragement to aim higher in life, irrespective of our choice of career. For that purpose, I recommend the following self-help and inspirational books from great authors whose books I have personally tasted.

- No Excuses: The Power of Self-Discipline by **Brian Tracy**
- You were born rich by **Bob Proctor**
- How to get from where you are to where you want to be by **Jack Canfield**
- Rest if you must but don't you quit by **Vic Johnson**
- You have a Brain by **Ben Carson**
- Maximum Achievement by **Brian Tracy**
- ABC of Success by **Bob Proctor**
- The Science of getting Rich by **Wallace D Wattles**
- Failure is never final by **Vic Johnson**
- The Success Principles by **Jack Canfield**
- The secret of the Ages by **Robert Collier**
- The Master Key System by **Charles Hannel**
- Your Invisible Power by **Genevieve Behrand**

- Psycho Cybernetics by **Maxwell Maltz**
- Feel the fear and do it anyway by **Susan Jeffers**
- The Magic of believing by **Claude M Bristol**
- My Philosophy for Successful living by **Jim Rohn**
- Think and Grow Rich by **Napoleon Hill**

About the Author

Anthony Oderinde is a Senior Consultant at Life Advancement Incorporation. He is an embodiment of God's riches with rigorous discipline of the academic.

He graduated with a First-class honours from Federal University of Technology, Akure, Nigeria, Distinction at Master's level from The University of Salford, United Kingdom. He is also a product of Innovative solutions and Creative thinking from Harvard, United States.

From personal experience and years of devoted studies, the Author has come to the realization of this important truth - "What gives a man or woman financial freedom or breakthrough in life is not a function of how many university degrees or certificates he or she possesses but in the understanding of some fundamental principles through which true riches and greatness could be attained".

This book "Intercourse with Superior Minds" is a means to these life changing principles. Regular intercourse with Superior Minds will unfold the fundamental principles and the application of the principles will bring riches in a mathematical exactitude and failure is impossible.

The journey to riches or greatness is an adventure and has its beginning in the understanding of the truth. No wonder the good book says "Ye shall know the truth and the truth shall set you free".

It is the truth, the real understanding of the principles of riches and greatness that can set us free from the prison and bondage of poverty and mediocrity.

www.ingramcontent.com/pod-product-compliance
Lightning Source LLC
Chambersburg PA
CBHW061748050726
47598CB00002B/634